# H.A.I.R. INFLUENCERS

*(Having Authority In Restoring)*

# H.A.I.R. INFLUENCERS

*(Having Authority In Restoring)*

Seven Powerpack Days of Hair-Restoring Declarations
A Comprehensive Guide in Declaring the Word of God
& Help Solve Your Hair Loss and Scalp Problem

## Shonda Roberts King

Xulon Press
2301 Lucien Way #415
Maitland, FL 32751
407.339.4217
www.xulonpress.com

*Note from the author:*

*Shonda R. King*
*Certified Trichologist*
*Hair Loss Practitioner*
*Holistic Practitioner*
*AMCA Certified*
*Master Cosmetologist*
*Gifted Creations Restoration Hair Loss Clinic*
*Giftedcreationshairlossclinic@gmail.com*
*WEB: www.giftedcreationssalon.com*

*Limitations of liability and disclaimer of warranty; while the publisher and author have used their best efforts in providing helpful and useful content in this book, they have no representation or warranties, with respect to the accuracy or completeness of the contents of this document and specifically disclaim any implied warranties of merchantability or fitness for particular purpose.*

*The advice and strategies contained therein may not be suitable for your situation. You should consult with a professional where appropriate. Neither the publisher nor author shall be liable for any loss of health, profit or any other commercial damages, including but not limited to special, incidental, consequential, or other damages.*

Paperback ISBN-13: 978-1-66282-789-1
Ebook ISBN-13: 978-1-66282-790-7

# DEDICATION

This book is dedicated with love to my parents, Alvin and Janice Roberts, as well as my grandparents, who are all smiling down from heaven: Willie Dillions, Simone Myers, Ella Roberts, and Corrine Law.

To my grandparents, Willie Dillions and Corrine Law: Thank you for all the years you made me plant your gardens. With me crying, because I would rather be playing with the kids, you would place the seeds in my hands, and you would say, "Just drop the seeds in the ground." I did not realize until I got older that your garden always had a great harvest. I cannot thank you both enough for those beautiful beginnings, and now these hands are helping grow thousands of hairs on the heads of women, men, and children all over the world.

To Grandma Ella, you would use the hot iron pressing comb on my hair like Madam C.J. Walker, because you knew I did not like going to the other lady, especially because of her roughness and from her burning me. Thank you for always rescuing me. Grandpa Simon, you went to heaven just when I was really getting to know you, but I will never forget your face, smile, and especially your love toward me.

And to all my clients that trusted me to care for you during your journey with hair loss, restoration of your hair or just hair care I truly thank you. To everyone that worked, trained or was mentored at Gifted Creations in these 25 years, we could not have assisted so many clients without you. We love and appreciate each of you.

And to all the women, men, and children who are suffering with hair loss and scalp disorders: Some suffer in silence and are not strong enough to speak or show it publicly. You keep it private and that is ok; just know you are beautiful. Do not allow anyone to make you feel different.

# Acknowledgments

I must thank God first, because, God, you know I can do nothing without You. You placed these gifts in me, and I cannot thank You enough for helping me write this book. I can only pray that this book, which is filled with Your Word, will impact others' lives as much, if not more, the way You have impacted my life.

To my incredibly supportive, my rock, my cheerleading husband, Melvin Jr. I cannot say thank you enough. Thank you for always pushing me to follow my dreams. You would never allow me to let circumstances or roadblocks stop me. You help me kick them down and re-focus, and you told me, as a team, "Let us make this happen." "I got you, babe" were your favorite words. These words gave me more strength to go even harder toward my goals.

You never judge me for coming up with ideas that seem so far out of our reach. You knew God was with us, and He most definitely was not going to let us fail. Honey, I love you with everything I have in me. You complete me, and I know God gave me the best in you. You helped me achieve my dreams and accomplish goals; and for this, I will always be grateful.

To my daughter, Chasity: Thank you for always being so honest. You made sure that I was more than alright. You are such an amazing and beautiful daughter. And you pushed me to go farther, always saying, "Mom, you can do it." And when you thought it was too much, you never held back in expressing, "Mom, no." That is what I love about you. I call you my solid rock, because you are that rock to me in so many ways. My butterfly you will always be. Thank you for your many sacrifices. I love and appreciate you beyond life.

To my son, Melvin III: Thank you for always pumping your mom up. You always made me feel like Superwoman, saying, "Mom, you can do it." You encourage me every step of the way. When things got hard, you would always say, "Mom, God got us and it's going to happen in God's timing." And, Son, you were right. The times I thought you forgot God's Word, you showed me, "Mom, I'll never forgot the Word of God." Thank you for being my greatest inspiration. I love you forever and ever, pass eternity.

To my sisters, Kendra Newton and Renada Garner, and brothers, Alvin Roberts, Willie Roberts and all my nieces and nephews: You all support me in so many ways. I cannot say thank you enough. I love you all so much; and I am grateful we have the greatest relationship in our own incredibly special and unique way. WE KNOW.LOL.

And to every client that trusted me with his or her hair loss or hair concerns: You allowed me to serve you with my gift. To every training class I have taken: Your classes gave me a greater understanding and knowledge about hair loss. I cannot name each one of you individually because I know me; I would miss someone and that would not be fair. I love you all so much.

And without prayer covering, none of this would be possible. My spiritual dad, Herbert Lambert: I think about you and miss you so much. You birthed some much in me. You gave me my solid foundation in believing every word of God. You taught me the crazy-faith, the just-believe-God-kind of faith; God is not a man but a spirit; And if you believe, than all things are possible. No matter what, God stands by His Word and He will stand by me. This is the only truth, so I believe God's Word.

Brother Emmanuel, you taught me about the supernatural miracle in knowing God and took my faith level to levels unknown. I love you both so much and am beyond thankful. You both are in heaven now, my guardian angels.

Apostle Dorothy and Pastor Algene Tanksley: You taught me how to fight with the Word and never give up. The Word of God is our weapon, and we always win. And to my mother, Janice Roberts: You taught me how to pray, pray without ceasing. For the prayers of the righteous avails much. To my dad Alvin Roberts thank you for being there whenever I needed you. To my second mom, Bessie King, God could not have given me a better second mom. To my family and friends' thanks for your love and support. I love you all so much and thank you again.

To those that always intercede for me, you know who you are. I love you so much. Thank you for being an ear and a knee to pray through things with me. I love you more than you will ever know.

# TABLE OF CONTENTS

# INTRODUCTION

**Combining the power of the word and hair growth is what I call,** *The Hair Influencer*.

*Hair* the bible declares that your Hair is your Glory. (1 Corinthians 11:15)

*Influencer* is someone who has the power to affect the decisions of others with authority, knowledge, position, or relationship with their audience. Following a distinct niche, with who, they are actively engaged.

If the Bible says, "If a woman has a good length hair it is her glory to her by God for a covering. If God calls hair a Glory, we should really care for this. Maintaining your hair is a gift from God.

We have the power to affect how your hair responds to our decisions and environment. Hair symbolizes, physical strength and vitality. The virtues and properties of a person are said to be concentrated in their hair. Your hair tells so many important factors about your life and health. Grey hair is a crown of splendor, it is attained in the way of righteousness. (Proverbs 16:31)

The word is clear, that hair is Gods gift to us. Gods word is health to our flesh. (Proverbs 4:22)

As long as we are willing to rely on Gods word, he promised he will be willing to meet every need; even something that would ordinarily seem inconsequential as Hair. I had to also learn and understand proper hair care.

How many times did it take for me to understand that when you try to accomplish things on your own, without the word of God, it could possibly fail? Not all the time did I fail alone because God said that there is safety in good counsel. It took me trying to figure that on my own sometimes delayed my progress. I had to understand the principals of what I was trying to learn and by understanding the principals it would alleviate a lot of the frustration. I made a commitment that it did not matter how hard or frustrating it got, I would continue trying until I found the answer/solution to hair loss. What I never did was give up, give in, or quit.

"THE ONLY WAY YOU ARE A FAILURE IS WHEN YOU QUIT!" And a quitter, I am not. I have led my life to believe that if you try, learn the principals and keep God first, you will never fail. You must understand what failure means; **failure** is the end of something, never going or moving forward again. To believe in and have a continued hoped in your dreams, visions and goals until it manifest is what compels me to keep going. This belief I hope to pass to my children(Chasity and Melvin), grand-daughter (Navi-Reign)my future grandchildren, and everyone that God places in my life.

The declarations are one of the most important part of my foundation God placed in my life. Thy word Oh God have I hid in my heart.

It is amazing how everything I needed in life, I found the answers and solutions in the Word of God and learning principals.

"Seek you first the Kingdom of God and everything else would be answered (added unto you)" (Matt. 6:33). I had to learn to apply the Word of God in my life, and afterwards I saw many benefits, answers, and the rewards that came from applying the word. The results which I experienced are unbelievable, overwhelming, and most beautiful for each client.

I know it may seem crazy, but I just believe I couldn't possibly do anything without God. His Word was truly the only FACT that never failed me. His Word made sense when nothing else in this world did, especially when I did not understand the reasons why people were losing their hair. Believe me, there were times in my life when I needed answers because I did not understand certain things that were happening. The only things that did not come short, did not change, were God and His Word. It worked 100 percent of the time when I applied God's Word correctly to situations. God said ask and he would give me understanding, wisdom and knowledge.

If you tried everything else and all have failed, I invite you to try declaring God's Word in your situation and see what you believe to manifest and stop worrying about your hair loss or anything.

One of my favorite Bible stories which shows you don't have to worry about anything is when Jesus was asleep on the boat in the middle of a storm with His disciples. His disciples were all afraid that they were going to be literally thrown off the boat and into the water. They had the nerve to ask Jesus, "How can you just sleep, and can you not see we are in the middle of a storm? Don't you care if we drown?" (Matt. 4:38). Jesus just opened His eyes, stood up, looked at the storm, and spoke three little words that changed the atmosphere and calmed the sea. Jesus said, "Peace be still" (Matt. 8:23-27). If the storm didn't disturb Jesus, why do we allow different storms of life to disturb our faith, beliefs, progress and even your hair loss?

If Jesus just used His word to speak directly to the situation, and the stormy sea immediately obeyed and calmed down, then I believe we can speak into our situations so the peace, answers, and solutions will surely change the circumstances. Just open your mouth and speak the Word of God. It's just as simple as learning to speak over yourself daily.

**Today declare these words**:
*I am the head and not the tail. Deuteronomy 28:13*
*I am above only and not beneath. Deuteronomy 28:13*
*I am healed by Jesus's stripes. Isaiah 53:5*
*I am a lender not a borrower. Deuteronomy 28:12*
*I owe no man nothing but to love them. Romans 13:8*
*I have everything I need. Philippians 4:18*
*I am prosperous and bless others out of my overflow.*
*2 Corinthians 9:8*

You can turn the following scriptures and decrees into prayers, along with taking proper care of your hair and health and watch your hair grow.

# Seven Days Hair-Restoring Declarations

"God says if I declare a thing it is established unto Me." (Job 22:28)

"I decided I will make it a habit to consciously speak life and watch my words to believe God. Because I know what he has for me shall come to pass.

"'You have observed correctly' said the LORD, 'for I am watching over MY word to accomplish it,' ......Then the LORD said to me, 'You have seen well, for I watch over my God word to perform it!'" (Jeremiah 1:12)

"If you are able to believe, EVERYTHING is possible to the one who believes." (Mark 9:23)

In life, we all have choices. We can choose to believe whatever we want; I made the choice to believe the Word of God and apply it to whatever I needed answers for. What did I have to lose? Either I am going to get what I believe or I am not. Believe me, most of my life I was learning to understand the principals and once I learned, my life became better.

You do not get in life what you **WANT**;
you get what you **BELIEVE**.
Oprah Winfrey
www.goodreads.com

When we go through adversity sometimes, we can forget that whatever happens in the negative can be restored. Hearing the Word of God is one of the most powerful things we can do and resting in what the Word says can bring about that restoration. This is good news because it means we no longer have to be sad or defeated by circumstances.

Fear is a weight that stops you from moving forward or even believing, but God's restoration means we do not have to be afraid. Whatever the circumstances, it is God's will to restore everything that was taken from us. The enemy can never defeat us, if we remember who we are and to whom we belong. So just try to remember you are never alone; you will make it and it will get better. Even if it's hair loss, just believe and it will get better.

Lastly, Don't Stress over it! The bible declares, "Do not be anxious about anything, but in everything by prayer and supplication with thanksgiving present your request to God. And the peace of God which transcends all understanding will guard your heart and mind in Christ Jesus. Philippians 4:6-7

# Seven Days of Declarations

## Day One

**Ecclesiastics 7:8 (NIV)**
"Better is the end of a thing than the beginning."

**Ecclesiastics 7:8 (MSG)**
"Endings are better than beginnings.
Sticking to it is better than standing out."

**Ecclesiastics 7:8 EHV**
"It is better to finish something than to begin something.
A patient spirit is better than a proud spirit."

**Ecclesiastics 7:8** ERV
"It is better to finish something than to start it. It is better to be gentle and patient than to the proud and impatient."

**Ecclesiastics 7:8** NLV
"The end of something is better than its beginning. Not giving up in spirit is better than being proud."

**Decree & Declare:**
Today, I will start my treatments and by the end of my hair and scalp treatments, I will have better results than my beginning treatments today. I believe that daily, my hair will get stronger and my scalp condition will improve. My eyes will see my desired results because I will not give up believing, and I have the patience it takes to go through the process. The Bible says, "Let patience have its perfect work" (Jas. 1:4). **I believe the Word of God spoken over me.**

## JOURNAL NOTES

What weekly regimens are you applying to your hair? Each week, your hair texture should become softer, smoother, and more vibrant with the right shampoo and conditioner. If not, I suggest you change your regimen.

_____

_____

_____

_____

_____

_____

_____

_____

_____

_____

_____

_____

_____

# DAY TWO

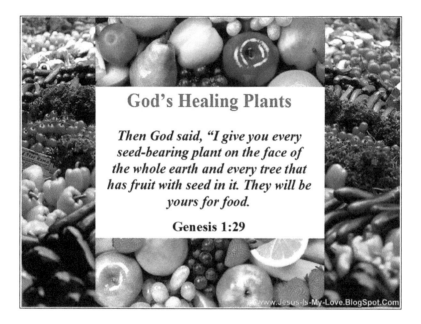

God's Healing Plants

*Then God said, "I give you every seed-bearing plant on the face of the whole earth and every tree that has fruit with seed in it. They will be yours for food.*

**Genesis 1:29**

www.Jesus-Is-My-Love.BlogSpot.Com

## Joel 2:25 KJV
"I will restore everything that the enemy has stolen."

## Joel 2:25 INT
"He can give us fruitful years as a compensation for those in which the locust ate up the fruits of the earth."

**Decree & Declare:**

Whatever the circumstances that may have caused me to lose my hair, I will not get frustrated because it is God's will to restore everything that was taken or destroyed (be it my hair follicles, my health, my joy, my peace, my self-confidence, my outer beauty, or my full head of hair). God will re-establish what the enemy stole or destroyed. My hair follicles will be fruitful and multiply. **I believe the Word of God spoken over me.**

## JOURNAL NOTES

What are you believing God to restore? Remember to believe is to have faith. Faith is hoping in what is not yet seen by the natural eye but having the assurance it will happen. (Hebrews 11:1)If you do not believe it's going to happen, then do not waste your time.

_____

_____

_____

_____

_____

_____

_____

_____

_____

_____

_____

_____

# DAY THREE 3

**Jeremiah 30:17 KJV**
"I will restore your health and heal your wounds,"
declares the Lord.

**Jeremiah 30:17 NET**
"Yes, I will restore you to health.
I will heal your wounds.
I, the LORD, affirm it!"

**Jeremiah 30:17 NIRV**
"'But I will make you healthy again.
I will heal your wounds,' announces the LORD."

**Jeremiah 30:17 NLV**
"For I will heal you. I will heal you where you have been
hurt,' says the Lord, 'because they have said that you are
not wanted.'"

**Decree & Declare:**
My body is healed of diabetes, thyroid (hyper or hypo), stress (mild or chronic), cancer, or any other sickness. God has healed all my wounds, whether in my metabolic system, endocrine system, cardiovascular system, skeletal system, etc. Anything in my entire body that is not performing effectively and efficiently is now healed and functioning at it best and fullest compacity. **I believe the Word of God spoken over me.**

## JOURNAL NOTES

Are you believing for healing? If so, where? Healing is not just physical but it could be also emotionally. What can you contribute to the healing process to ensure you will receive your healing?

_____

_____

_____

_____

_____

_____

_____

_____

_____

_____

_____

_____

_____

# Day Four 4

**Luke 21:18** KJV
"Never! As surely as the Lord lives, not a hair of your head will fall to the ground!"

**Matthew 10:30** AMP
"But even the very hairs of your head are all numbered [for the Father is sovereign and has complete knowledge]."

**Matthew 10:30** ERV
"God even knows how many hairs are on your head."

**Matthew 10:30** CEV
"Even the hairs on your head are counted."

**Decree & Declare:**
I believe God lives, and God said not a hair on my head will fall to the ground. So, as I do my part by eating healthy, taking my nutrients if needed, drinking water, exercising, relaxing and not stressing, and speaking the Word of God, I will see the results and all these benefits of having not lost

another strand of my hair. I'm believing for a head full of hair. **I believe the Word of God spoken over me.**

## JOURNAL NOTES

When you find yourself stressing, what can you do to eliminate the stress in your life? Stress is carrying the weight of things you cannot control. Breathe and let it go.

_____

_____

_____

_____

_____

_____

_____

_____

_____

_____

_____

_____

_____

# DAY FIVE

**1 Samuel 14:45**
"Never! As surely as the LORD lives, not a hair of his head will fall to the ground, for with God's help he has accomplished this today."

**1 Samuel 14:45** CBS
"No, as the LORD lives, not a hair of his head will fall to the ground, for he worked with God's help today."

**1 Samuel 14:45** GW
"That would be unthinkable! We solemnly swear, as the LORD lives, not a single hair of his head will fall to the ground, because he has done this with God's help today."

**1 Samuel 14:45** KJV
"God forbid: as the LORD liveth, there shall not one hair of his head fall to the ground; for he hath wrought with God this day."

**1 Samuel 14:45** MSG
"As surely as GOD lives, not a hair on his head is going to be harmed. Why, he's been working hand-in-hand with God all day!"

**Decree & Declare:**
Today, I may be facing a challenge or struggling to see what I want today, but with God's help and His grace, I will accomplish and see my prayers answered in faith. I shall see it all become better. Today, I am better. I receive strength, joy, and peace that my health and hair is getting stronger and longer every day. My mind and heart are at peace. **I believe the Word of God spoken over me.**

## JOURNAL NOTES

We all have our personal challenges. What are some personal challenges that you would love to overcome? And what plan of action can you take to overcome these challenges?

_____

_____

_____

_____

_____

_____

_____

_____

_____

_____

_____

_____

_____

_____

_____

_____

_____

_____

_____

_____

_____

_____

_____

_____

_____

_____

_____

_____

# Day six 6

**Mark 11:24**

"Therefore I say to you, all things for which you pray and ask, believe that you have received them, and they will be granted."

**Mark 11:24 MSG**

"Jesus was matter-of-fact: 'Embrace this God-life. Really embrace it, and nothing will be too much for you. This mountain, for instance: Just say, "Go jump in the lake"—no shuffling or shilly-shallying—and it is as good as done. That is why I urge you to pray for absolutely everything, ranging from small to large. Include everything as you embrace this God-life, and you will get God's everything. And when you assume the posture of prayer, remember that it is not all *asking*."

**Mark 11:24 *KJV***

"Therefore, I say unto you, what things soever ye desire, when ye pray, believe that ye receive them, and ye shall have them."

**Mark 11:24 ISV**

"That is why I tell you, whatever you ask for in prayer, believe that you have received[a] it and it will be yours."

**Mark 11:24 NET**

"For this reason, I tell you, whatever you pray and ask for, believe that you have received it, and it will be yours."

**Decree & Declare:**

I pray and ask that my hair go from the telogen phase, where my hair growth RESTED/STOP BUT remained active, into the anagen stage. This stage allows my hair to grow and get stronger and longer every day. I shall receive and see at least a fourth of an inch of new hair growing every twenty-eight days OR LESS. I believe everything that has paused, rested, or stopped in my life will be activated now in this season.

**I believe the Word of God spoken over me.**

## JOURNAL NOTES

What has stopped in your life that you are believing God to start again? What do you believe caused it to stop? The key is not to blame people, so true healing can began.

_____

_____

_____

_____

_____

_____

_____

_____

_____

_____

_____

_____

# DAY SEVEN

**Ephesians 3:20 KJV**
"God will do exceedingly abundantly above all you can ask think or imagine."

**Ephesians 3:20 NET**
"Now to him who by the power that is working within us[a] is able to do far beyond[b] all that we ask or think."

**Ephesians 3:20 NIV**
"Now to him who is able to do immeasurably more than all we ask or imagine, according to his power that is at work within you."

**Ephesians 3:20 MSG**
"God can do anything, you know—far more than you could ever imagine or guess or request in your wildest dreams! He does it not by pushing us around but by working within us, his Spirit deeply and gently within us."

**Ephesians 3:20 ISV**
"Now to the one who can do infinitely more than all we can ask or imagine according to the power that is working among[a] us."

**Decree & Declare:**
God, I thank you that I am seeing and receiving greater results than I thought I would. I see great hair growth; my hair loss has decreased. My scalp and hair are healthy. The position of hair loss has now become smaller, and every day I am seeing greater and better results in my hair growth. My edges are full, and the top crown of my hair is getting fuller every day. I see my hair growing like never before; I told myself that it would happen, and I am seeing the evidence now. I will rise above this situation. **I believe the Word of God spoken over me.**

## JOURNAL NOTES

What are the obstacles you want to overcome and believe for? Are these obstacles internal or external? I believe the hardest obstacles are those that only you know about and are trying to hide. Your healing can begin when you learn to let it go.

_____

_____

_____

_____

_____

_____

_____

_____

_____

_____

_____

_____

# It's Manifestation Time

**Decree & Declare:**
**I am seeing all that I hoped for. My hair is fully restored.**
**I feel like I am dreaming, but it's real. I can NOT stop**
**singing and laughing. IT'S REAL! The Lord has done**
**great things for my hair, my health, my self-esteem,**
**my confidence, and my life! I believe the Word of God**
**spoken over me.**

I realized that words are powerful. If you speak it enough,
it will happen!

God has given us instructions to live by; clear instructions on how to have a life where there is nothing missing,
lacking, or broken. But so many times, I pick and choose
what I want and how I want to follow out these instructions.

If I had to do it all over again, I would not deviate from the instructions; it only prolonged the process.

Yes, I believe we all want the best life and the best of life! But unfortunately, our lives do not reflect what we are speaking out of our mouths. We do not realize the words we speak have power; power to manifest! It's real power to make things happen as though they should be! And not only our words, but our actions and decisions have shaped our lives. So now, even if you do not see it right now in this very moment, learn to speak it. Keep speaking it because those words are seeds shaping your life and future to become good and beautiful.

**Decide to be intentional with what you speak!**

**Secret** that I had to learn and share:

I only focus, only speak, on the things I want and desire. I give no energy to the things I do not want. The secret is watch how things shift after this determination!

Why did I choose seven days and not twenty-one or thirty days of hair-restoring declarations? I know we were told if you did something for twenty-one days, it would become a permanent habit. I realize that not only I but some of my clients were more consistent in short-term goals. I also realize that repetition gave us greater results. These little instructions allowed me to master the strategy, so declare the word for seven days and three weeks consistently is one of my recommendations. Therefore a consistent routine helps to complete and accomplish the goals that were set. And besides that, the greater plan was to line up with God's Word, use His principles (eating healthy) and my God-given knowledge about hair loss and many saw lifechanging results.

God made the world in six days and rested on the seventh. This entire world was created and replenished with everything it needed to prosper and be sufficient in six days. When God finished, He sat back and said this is good! This is good! God did all that in only six days! So, if God could get all that done in six days, surely, we can get a portion of good results if we are consistent.

# Just Remember

"A peaceful heart brings a healthy body."
**(Proverbs 14:30)**

"The fear of the Lord leads to life than one rest, content and untouched by trouble." **(Proverbs 19:23)NIV**

Use your authority; do not fear!

Quitting, giving up, or going back to doing nothing is never an option. We will see the greater in your hair -recovery journey.

"Do not throw away your confidence because it has great reward. You have need of endurance, because when you have done the will of God you may receive what was promised." (Hebrews 10:35,NKJV)

"Do not throw it all away now. You were sure of yourself then. It is still a sure thing. You need to stick it out staying with God's plan so you will be there for the promise completion." (Hebrews 10:35)MSG

It will not be long now; it is on the way. Your blessing will show up any minute!

But we are not quitters who lose out! Oh no! I will stay with it and survive, trusting all the way.

# You Got To Work It

"So too, faith by itself, if it does NOT result in ACTION, is dead." James 2:17

When choosing a product that will allow you to maintain or condition the hair to become better, it is so important to choose wisely. I could not find a verse in the Bible, but I found these in the forgotten books of Adam and Eve listed below.

**Shampoo and Conditioner**

**Seth 9:10-12** four is a man or woman finds a good shampoo, he has found a good thing. Anne will be received into the king, for good hair is better than silver and gold curly buns, better than a nagging and annoying spouse.

**Rehoboam 6**:2-4:

And Pharaoh said to his maid servant, "Fetch me shampoo," and his maidservant immediately ran off to fetch him shampoo. And as the pharaoh applied the shampoo on his hair, he lifted his eyes and gazed upon the Nile; and behold a voice said to him, "Does it smell nice and all good, Pharaoh?" And he replied, "Yes it does. It smells better than any of my garden of roses."

You must choose wisely the proper shampoo and conditioner that meet your specific hair type and texture. Depending on the circumstances or challenges you may be dealing with, concerning your scalp or hair, you may have to shampoo in as little as every two days (extreme cases) or at least a minimum of every seven to ten days (healthy cases).

Another tip is understanding what your hair type and texture is.

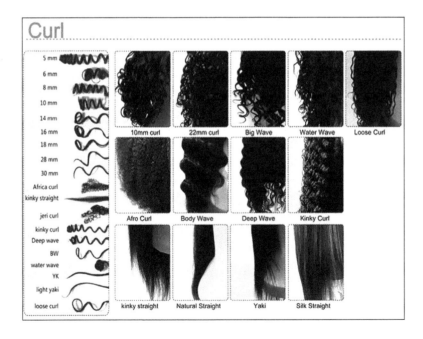

**When considering the choice of a shampoo:** When your hair and scalp are dry, you do not want to choose a shampoo that is made **ONLY** to deep cleanse. This shampoo is not going to give your hair the benefits it is requiring or give your hair the nourishment it needs to become healthy and perform at its best. On the flip side of this equation, you do not want to choose a shampoo that is designed **only** to give you moisture, if your hair and/or scalp is always oily. This too is preventing your hair type and/or texture to receive the benefits it needs to perform at its ultimate best.

You can always do your own research. Reach out to your master cosmetologist or email me at giftedcreationsalon@gmail.com, for help.

Conditioners are used to improve the feel, appearance, and manageability of hair. Its main purpose is to reduce friction between strands of hair to allow smoother brushing or combing, which might otherwise cause damage to the scalp. Various other benefits can happen, such as hair repair, strengthening, or a reduction in split ends, when using conditioners.

Just like when choosing a shampoo, how often you are applying the conditioner to your hair depends upon the severity or condition of your hair. If your hair is severely dry, rough in feel, and/or doesn't shine, you would be conditioning more often than someone's hair who is healthy, shiny, and has vibrancy.

# You Are What You Eat

"That each of them may eat and drink and find satisfaction in all their toil—this is the gift of God." Ecclesiastes 3:13

Food is a gift from God. We use it to celebrate, to mourn, to entertain, to fuel, to love, to show hospitality, and to care for people in tangible ways. There are definitely dangers to overeating (just as there are to undereating), but we need food daily. We must understand balance, as there is a balance in everything we chose to put inside our bodies. If we chose wisely, I believe we will have lives that resemble those choices. And more times than we care to count, we misuse the healthier choices of food.

Food affects every aspect of our being: mood, energy levels, food cravings, thinking capacity, sex drive, sleeping habits, and, mostly, our general health. If we feed our bodies junk food, they will produce bad fat, lowering our energy and even our brain power. When we do not supply our bodies with the healthy choice of foods, we deplete our bodies of the nutrients they need to function effectively and thrive.

When our bodies are not functioning properly, they suffer. And this one way may be the cause of so many losing their hair and having health issues. I had to decide that I must make the better choices for my hair and health.

# Fun Food Quiz

Choose which foods are the better choices and what time of day would be best to eat them. Which one would you eliminate from your life?

**\*Choose Good Foods**          **\*Eliminate Bad Foods**

**\*Morning**          **\*Lunch**          **\*Dinner**          **\*Snacks**

ALMONDS  BLUEBERRIES  CHICKEN  FISH  LENTILS
PIZZA  PEACH COBBLER  APPLES  RAISINS  OATMEAL  PASTA
RICE  CEREAL  FRUIT SNACKS  CANDY  LIMA BEANS  HAM
TURKEY  LAMB  PORKCHOPS  ELK  CHEESE  EGGS  GRITS
CANNED GOODS  HAMBURGERS  FRENCH FRIES  SALAD
PANCAKES  WAFFLES  SANDWICH MEATS  WHITE BREAD
BACON  FRIED CHICKEN  GRILLED CHEESE SANDWICH
STRAWBERRIES  ORANGES  GRAPEFRUIT  RICE NOODLES
WATERMELON  GRAPES  KALE  SPINACH  OXTAILS
WATER  SODA/RED BULL  SWEET TEA  GREEN TEA
LEMONS  VINIGAR  SUGAR  OATMEAL  PIE  NUTS  WINE

# Build Your Daily
# Healthy Meal Plan

## SUNDAY

### BREAKFAST

- _____
- _____
- _____

### LUNCH

- _____
- _____
- _____

## SNACK

- _____
- _____
- _____

## DINNER

- _____
- _____
- _____

"So whether you eat or drink or whatever you do, do it all for the glory of God." – 1 Corinthians 10:31

# MONDAY

## BREAKFAST

- _____
- _____
- _____

## LUNCH

- _____
- _____
- _____

## SNACK

- _____

- _____

- _____

## DINNER

- _____

- _____

- _____

"It is not good to eat too much honey, nor is it honorable to search out matters that are too deep." – Proverbs 25:27

## TUESDAY

### BREAKFAST

- _____
- _____
- _____

### LUNCH

- _____
- _____
- _____

## SNACK

- _____
- _____
- _____

## DINNER

- _____
- _____
- _____

"I have the right to do anything," you say—but not everything is beneficial. "I have the right to do anything"—but I will not be mastered by anything. – 1 Corinthians 6:12

## WEDNESDAY

### BREAKFAST

- _____
- _____
- _____

### LUNCH

- _____
- _____
- _____

## SNACK

- _____
- _____
- _____

## DINNER

- _____
- _____
- _____

"That each of them may eat and drink, and find satisfaction in all their toil—this is the gift of God." – Ecclesiastes 3:13

# THURSDAY

## BREAKFAST

- _____
- _____
- _____

## LUNCH

- _____
- _____
- _____

## SNACK

- _____
- _____
- _____

## DINNER

- _____
- _____
- _____

"No temptation has overtaken you that is not common to man. God is faithful, and he will not let you be tempted beyond your ability, but with the temptation, he will also provide the way of escape, that you may be able to endure it." – 1 Corinthians 10:13

# FRIDAY

## BREAKFAST

- _____
- _____
- _____

## LUNCH

- _____
- _____
- _____

## SNACK

- _____
- _____
- _____

## DINNER

- _____
- _____
- _____

**CHOOSING TO EAT HEALTHY IS CHOOSING TO LIVE BETTER AND LIVE HAPPIER AND HEALTHY.**

## SATURDAY

### BREAKFAST

- _____
- _____
- _____

### LUNCH

- _____
- _____
- _____

## SNACK

- _____
- _____
- _____

## DINNER

- _____
- _____
- _____

**A GENEROUS PERSON WILL BE BLESSED, FOR HE SHARES HIS FOOD.**

**WHEN I LOOK AT MYSELF IN THE MIRROR, I LOOK AT THE BEST OF ME. I CHOSE TO EAT HEALTHY AND LIVE BEAUTIFULLY.**

# Foods and its Benefits

**Almonds** provide plenty of nutrients, including: magnesium, vitamin E, iron, calcium, fiber, riboflavin

**Blueberries** are rich in calcium, iron, magnesium, phosphorus, zinc, and vitamin K, which all work to **strengthen bones and maintain bone structure**.

**Brazil Nuts** are excellent sources of both protein and carbohydrates, and they also provide good amounts of vitamin B-1, vitamin E, magnesium, and zinc.

Brazil nuts also contain more selenium than many other foods. Selenium is a vital mineral for maintaining thyroid function, and it is a great antioxidant for the human body.

These nuts come in a hard shell and are usually available ready to eat, making them a quick, nutritious snack.

**Lentils** provide good amounts of fiber, magnesium, and potassium.

They tend to require a long cooking time. However, manufacturers can sprout the seeds, making them a delicious, healthful, and ready-to-eat snack.

Adding a container of sprouted lentils to a lunchbox or picnic basket, perhaps with some chili powder or pepper for flavoring, makes for a delicious and healthful snack.

**Oatmeal Oats** contain complex carbohydrates, as well as water-soluble fiber. These slow down digestion and help stabilize levels of blood glucose. Oatmeal is also a good source of folate and potassium.

**Wheat germ** is high in several vital nutrients, including fiber, vitamin E, folic acid, thiamin, zinc, magnesium, phosphorus, fatty alcohols, and essential fatty acids.

**Fruits, vegetables, and berries** are easy to incorporate into the diet. The following are some of the most healthy:

**Broccoli** provides good amounts of fiber, calcium, potassium, folate, and phytonutrients. Phytonutrients are compounds that reduce the risk of developing heart disease, diabetes, and some cancers.

Broccoli also provides essential antioxidants, such as vitamin C and beta-carotene. In fact, a single half-cup serving of broccoli can provide around 85 percent of a person's daily vitamin C.

Another compound in broccoli called sulforaphane may have anticancer and anti-inflammatory.

However, overcooking broccoli can destroy many of its key nutrients. For this reason, it is best to eat it raw or lightly steamed.

**Apples** are an excellent source of antioxidants, which combat free radicals. Free radicals are damaging substances that the body generates. They cause undesirable changes in the body and may contribute to chronic conditions, as well as the aging process.

However, some studies have suggested that an antioxidant in apples might extend a person's life span and reduce the risk of chronic disease.

**Kale** is a leafy green vegetable that offers a wide range of different nutrients. For example, this powerfully nutritious plant is an excellent source of vitamins C and K.

People can cook or steam kale. They can also blend it into smoothies or juices for a nutritional kick.

**Blueberries** has an impact on bone health. They are rich in calcium, iron, magnesium, zinc, phosphorus, and vitamin K, which all work to strengthen bones and maintain bone structure.

They are low in calories and incredibly healthy, potentially regulating blood sugar levels and aiding heart and brain health.

Often marketed as a superfood, blueberries are an excellent source of several vitamins, beneficial plant compounds, and antioxidants.

**Avocados** are avoided sometimes by people due to their high fat content. However, avocados provide healthful fats, as well as B vitamins, vitamin K, and vitamin E. Avocados are also a good source of fiber.

Avocados increased levels of high-density lipoprotein, or "good" cholesterol. This type of cholesterol removes more harmful cholesterol from the bloodstream.

Avocados might also have anti-cancer properties. Colored avocado seed extract reduced the viability of breast, colon, and prostate cancer cells.

Avocados may also have associations with improved nutrient absorption, better overall diet, and fewer metabolic risk factors.

**Leafy greens**: Spinach is an example of a leafy green with antioxidant content, especially when it is raw, steamed, or very lightly boiled. It is a good source of the following nutrients: vitamins A, B-6, C, E, and K, selenium, niacin, zinc, phosphorus, copper, potassium, calcium, manganese, betaine, and iron.

**Sweet potatoes** provide dietary fiber, vitamin A, vitamin C, vitamin B-6, and potassium.

Sweet potatoes ranked number one for their vitamin A, vitamin C, iron, calcium, protein, and complex carbohydrate content.

**Fish:** some examples of oily fish include salmon, trout, mackerel, herring, sardines, and anchovies. These types of fish have oil in their tissues and around their gut.

Their lean fillets contain high levels of omega-3 fatty acids. These oils may provide benefits for the heart and nervous systems.

Suggest that omega-3 fatty acids can help with inflammatory conditions, such as arthritis. They are also plentiful in vitamins A and D.

**Chicken** is a cost-effective and healthful meat. Free-range chicken serves as an excellent source of protein.

However, it is important to remember that preparation and cooking methods affect how healthful chicken is. This means that people should limit their intake of deep-fried chicken and always remove the skin before consumption. Chicken skin has high levels of saturated fat.

**Eggs** are another source of protein that people can easily incorporate into a balanced diet, as they are highly versatile.

Eggs contain vitamins including B-2 and B-12, both of which are important for preserving energy and generating red blood cells. Eggs are also a good source of the essential amino acid leucine, which plays a role in stimulating muscle protein synthesis. Eggs also provide a good amount of choline, which is important for cell membranes.

The yolk contains most of the egg's vitamins and minerals, as well as the fat and cholesterol.

# Why I Care about Hair Loss and Clients' Testimonies

My passion is always wanting to help, be a problem-solver and not the cause of the problem. I believe I have been in business probably ten years as a master cosmetologist when I saw my career shifting. My clients were becoming older, and I saw that things were changing with a few of my clients' hair. I had to figure out why these clients were losing their hair. I became a certified trichologist, with many years of training and with all the years of experience. It allowed me to have a better understanding of hair loss and to provide hair -loss solutions that worked.

I was able to see how hair loss affected people in so many ways, with some of it causing depression, anxiety, embarrassment, lower self-esteem, etc. Regaining the hair that was lost, and even stopping the progression of losing more hair, was priceless. The clients' smiles and self-confidence were worth any dollar spent.

I understand the saying, "A picture is worth a thousand words." Sometimes you do not have to say anything; just look at the proof or, some would say, the evidence.

# Client Testimonies

I started this journey in 2014 with Gifted Creations Salon. I did not know what the future years would hold for me as I embark on this transformation, but I am truly thankful for these ladies, Shonda and Chasity King.

When I started this, I was totally in denial about my hair. I thought I had length and that is all that I needed. However, I quickly learned that my hair was not healthy, and it was just hanging on. So, I begin this process and each hair appointment, faithfully every two weeks, my hair continued to amaze me. I was now a believer in what my cosmetologist was doing to my hair. It became healthier and my length has surpassed from where I started. Gifted Creations has completely changed my life and my confidence to wear my natural hair. I thank God for them every day.

Love a faithful client always,
Charlese Kennedy

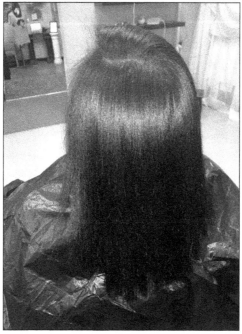

Gifted Creations is like one of the seven wonders of the world. Shonda King is amazing with her hair products *Naturally Redeemed*. Her hair products have worked amazing results in my hair. My hair was a short boy haircut; now my hair is halfway down my back. I am so amazed with the knowledge she has. She is so caring. If I should ever leave this area, I will travel for her to do my hair. She will always be my stylist. She not only cares about your hair; she cares about you as a person.

Carol Fletcher

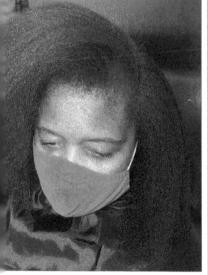

It was **August 2010** when I started my natural hair journey. I always had a relaxer that ended up damaging my hair and had lot of breakage. Once I was referred to Mrs. Shonda King, my journey to natural health hair began. I didn't do the big chop; I just transitioned from relaxed hair to natural hair. Once my journey began, I only used her products. My length of my hair was basically a bob when I first started going to Gifted Creations. Her products and her time with developing my hair to being healthy and natural are amazing. Her products are wonderful and helped my hair to stay healthy and manageable. I recommend all her hair care line (*Naturally Redeemed*) and services that she provides for healthy, natural hair.

Jasmine Haynes

For years, I believed my hair would grow a certain length, then break off every fall season. After meeting Shonda and Chasity, I was reassured my hair would grow and be healthier than it's ever been. "Your hair is in my hands," said Shonda. From that point to eight years later, my hair is thicker, longer, and more beautiful! Thank you Gifted Creations!

Rebecca Mock

I have been going to Gifted Creations for about eighteen months. When I first started, my hair was truly short and very brittle; so short on the sides that two strand twists weren't possible. The pictures clearly show how healthy my hair is now and how much my hair has grown. I am extremely appreciative of Shonda's hair-care expertise.

Stascia Hardy

Going through cancer is more than some can handle. But I'm grateful she trusted me through the entire process. We saw that you can totally recovery from losing all your hair to regaining every strain back. The hair returned stronger and we kept it healthy.

Shonda King

After being frustrated with the ongoing struggles with my hair, I learned of Gifted Creations through my braider. My braider spoke highly of their professionalism. She provided me with their website. I immediately pulled up their page and was amazed that their salon, Gifted Creations Salon in Midway, Georgia, was featured in *Essence Magazine*; that they had sold products Michelle Obama used on her hair. I made my first appointment. It was nothing shy of AMAZING!! Fast forward, six to eight months of transitioning my hair, it was growing but the relaxed hair continued to hang on. The turning point was when I decided to allow Mrs. Shonda and Ms. Chasity to do a "big chop." They cheered me on and assured that it would make a major change in my healthy hair journey. The routine visits to Gifted Creations and usage of their special hair line is a reflection of my current hair growth. They are truly God-sent!!

Thank you,
Angel Tumbling

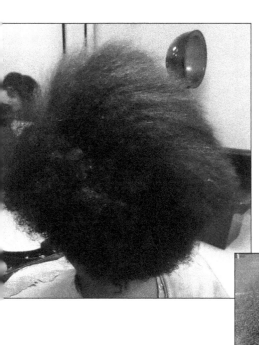

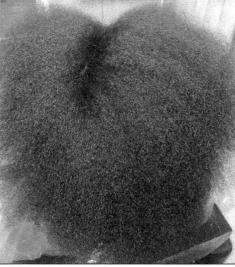

My hair journey with Gifted Creation Salon begin June 2019. I was very frustrated. My hair was in a complete natural state, not by choice. My hair was thinning and could not tolerate hair relaxers. A very good friend referred me to Shonda and Chasity. They were the miracle I was looking for. My scalp and hair was evaluated. I was place a hair regiment. As you can see through the pictures of the beginning, year 1 , year and 2, all in the month of June, I found the miracle I needed. After year 1, I was allowed to received color. The hair regiment consists of the special hair products used at Gifted Creation. I have received so many compliments about my hair. I am constantly referring people to Gifted Creation Salon. I want everyone to experience the miracle I am receiving!

Deborah Covington

# MORE TESTIMONIES...

 **Stephanie Allen** 💬 recommends
**Gifted Creations Salon.**
Jun 20, 2017 · 🌐

Gifted Creations Salon is the best!! I have been coming here for 15+ years. When I moved out of the area, I tried several other salons, but could not find any who were able to care for my hair like Gifted Creations. The drive is definitely worth it!! Shonda and Chasity are AWESOME!! They restore my hair in salon and give me tips and products for home care. Anddddd they offer services for makeup, nails and massages! #OneStopShop

**Elisha-Lisa Gaskins** 💬 recommends
**Gifted Creations Salon.**
May 22, 2019 · 🌐

Hey sis!!! Just wanted to let you know that since we have been using your products on Justice hair that she hasn't had any dry patches in months!!! I will be reordering very soon!!! 🖤
🖤🖤🖤🖤🖤🖤

**Amazing results**

**Tee Bee** 💬 recommends **Gifted Creations Salon.**
May 7 at 10:34 AM · 🌐

I love the friendliness of the staff for starters. I am very pleased with my hair do as well. Usually I find some type of fault after the stylist finishes with my hair but not this time. It looks so healthy and refresh. Any time I have seen someone hair that I like, they said Shonda at Gifted Creations done it. I will be returning. Also I thought the price was reasonable for deep conditioning, trim and style.

**Deliza Jones** 💬 recommends **Gifted Creations Salon.**
May 1 at 10:56 AM · 🌐

My hair was so far gone from over processing, my co workers recommended me to this salon she had been going to for years because I wanted someone who worked well with natural hair like mine. These ladies did NOT disappoint in the least!! I'm rocking a new cute hair style with healthy hair. And their products (made themselves btw) are also amazing on my curls!! Very homey and I refuse to go to anyone else now that I've discovered these gems!!

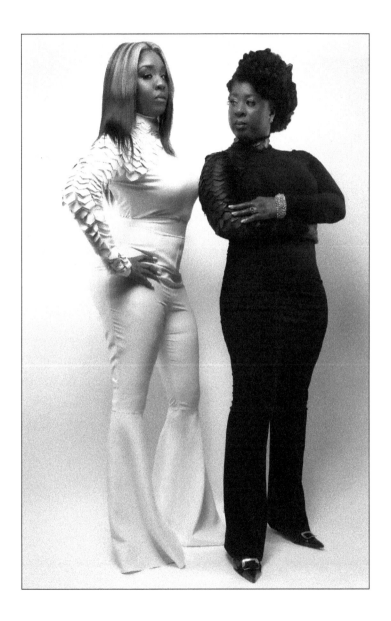

Shonda & Chasity King
Mom and Daughter Duo Gifted Creations Salon

# My Prayer

I pray that the God I serve, the one and only true living God, would bless each person that reads this book. I pray you will know that He is God who supplies all your needs (Phil. 4:19). It does not matter if it is mental, financial, social, or in your family, health, marriage, life, and even for your hair to grow. Know that the Word of God will never return to you void (Isa. 55:11). God stands and watches over His Word to perform every word that comes forth out of your mouth. For the Word of God will NEVER fail (Lk. 1:37).

I pray God will bless you exceedingly abundantly above all you could ever think or imagine (Eph. 3:11). Know that it does not matter what has happened in your life and what you think you may have missed, or you were not good enough for. The reality of the matter is, KNOW that the PLAN of God will always prevail in your life (Jer. 29:11).

God bless,
SHONDA KING

WE ARE H.A.I.R. INFLUENCERS SISTERS
(Have Authority In Righteousness)
To Join www.hairinfluencers8@gmail.com

CPSIA information can be obtained
at www.ICGtesting.com
Printed in the USA
BVHW060843011121
620445BV00020B/707